PASTOR POTTER'S POINTS
Volume II.

Ellis Potter

© 2021 ELLIS POTTER

Without limiting the rights under copyright reserved above, no part of this publication may be reproduced, stored in, or introduced into a retrieval system, or transmitted in any form or by any means (electronic, mechanical, photocopying, or otherwise), without the prior written permission from the publisher, except where permitted by law, and except in the case of brief quotations embodied in critical articles and reviews. For information, write: info@destineemedia.com

Reasonable care has been taken to trace original sources and copyright holders for any quotations appearing in this book. Should any attribution be found to be incorrect or incomplete, the publisher welcomes written documentation supporting correction for subsequent printing.

Published by: Destinée Media
www.destineemedia.com

Cover design by Peter Wonson
Cover and interior by Istvan Szabo, Ifj.
Formatting by Istvan Szabo, Ifj.

All rights reserved by the author.
ISBN 978-1-938367-66-3

Table of Contents

Introduction 8
90% >100% 10
200% Reality 11
A Parable of Hurt and Healing 12
Amen 13
Angels 14
Anger and Paranoia 15
Attachment and Freedom 16
Be at Peace or Don't Care? 17
Beauty 18
Blasphemy 19
Calling 20
Cause and Effect 21
Chance 22
Christian Patriotism 23
Christianity is Ordinary 24
Citizenship in Heaven 25
Civil Disobedience 26
Comfort 27
Communion 28

Controversial	29
Covenant	30
Culture	31
Cyberspace	32
Draw Near to God	33
Earth, Air, Fire and Water	34
Entertainment and Education	35
Equality	36
Fasting	37
Follow Your Heart	38
Freedom to Fail	39
Fundamentalism	40
Give Thanks in All Circumstances	41
God's Law of Love	42
God's Promises	43
Grace	44
Hallowed Be Thy Name	45
Holy Selfishness	46
Hospitality	47
How We Know	48
I Don't Know	49
"I Know What I Like."	50

Information	51
Investing in Prayer	52
Jesus is the Answer	53
Justice and Love	54
Learning from Our Emotions	55
Limits of Freedom	56
Love and Trust	57
Loving Our Neighbor is Loving God	58
Luck	59
Male and Female	60
Meaning of Meaning	61
Migration	62
Mistrust	63
Needy	64
Nothing is Safe	65
Ocean	66
One, Two or Three?	67
Our Brother's Keeper	68
Parable of a Victim	69
People are Good	70
Personal Goodness	71
Prayer and Bicycle Riding	72

Predestination	73
Pride	74
Questions as Blessings	75
Race	76
Reading and Listening	77
Relevant	78
Religion or Idolatry	79
Religion	80
Restrictions	81
Revelation	82
Righteousness	83
Risk and Trust	84
Self-Referential	85
Spiritual Activities	86
"Spiritual" Connections	87
Test Everything	88
Testing and Tempting	89
The Desires of Our Hearts	90
The End is Near!	91
The Parable of the Mother and the Boy	92
The Problem of Evil	93
The Problem of Good	94

The Spirit Blows and Hovers 95
The Temple of the Holy Spirit 96
Trust and Confidence 97
Trust and Panic 98
Two Kinds of People 99
Unconditional Love 100
Understanding God's Word 101
Value and Desire 102
Victory During Covid 103
Wanting What God Wants 104
What About Those Who Have Never
   Heard? (Part I) 105
What About Those Who Have Never
   Heard? (Part II) 106
Why? 107
Wisdom 108
Words and Feelings 109

Introduction

The Covid virus restrictions have continued into 2021, so the daily emails to the Church in Lausanne where I pastor have also continued. Each email had Bible passages for reading together and a pastoral thought or point, which have been collected to make this second book of 100 points.

These points are mostly original with me and some I have read and adapted, adding my own angle or application. They can be used as a daily dose for meditation or for group discussions in any order or grouping you choose.

The book is 100 points in 100 words on 100 pages. You can read one page each day for over three months and then start over.

The points are uneven in their importance, breadth, and depth. Depending on your condition and situation, some of the "lesser" points might be most important. The points are very brief and much more needs to be said about them. They are starting points.

The points are compressed to fit into one paragraph of about 100 words each. They need to be read like a prose poem or extended Haiku.

Many of these points were developed because of questions people asked. Some of the points will be familiar or obvious to you. Some might be new.

Not everyone will agree with all the points. Do not stress, just think and pray about them. Or write a better point on the same topic. Many of the points are based on Bible study but the references are not given as there are often too many. The points are Biblical but not very denominational or political in orientation.

Some of these points are found in the content of my other books.

Ellis Potter, Basel 2021

90% >100%

"90% is greater than 100%" is not a true equation in space time mathematics. It is wonderfully true in the Kingdom of God. Tithing is not commanded in the New Testament but giving generously and cheerfully is. Setting aside 10% of our income (gross or net) for giving away, regularly or spontaneously, is an eternal investment for us. It also seems mysteriously to bring Peace and financial security here and now. Many Christians are afraid to do this because their faith is weak. Don't think of it as a sacrifice. Think of it as an investment. Try it.

200% Reality

Naturalistic science has taught us to understand reality in terms of 100%. But if we put things like God's Sovereignty and people's free will on a two-dimensional pie chart it never divides up well. We end up with no sovereignty or no free will. The Bible adds a 100% supernatural reality. If we use a three-dimensional sphere chart, we can see a 100% plane of Sovereignty and a 100% plane of free will. Sovereignty and free don't compete for space, they complement each other in a marriage relationship. Christians are not equal to God. They are 100% committed.

A Parable of Hurt and Healing

Once there was a little girl who was hurt, rejected and bullied in various ways. She built a wall around herself and effectively shut out the pain. Her highest priority was to avoid pain. Loneliness, anxieties, fears and other problems developed. She was unhappy and unwell. Then she realized she had been trying to be her own God and protector and had crippled herself. She turned to God in confession and was forgiven. She turned to God in trust for protection and true identity in Jesus Christ and the healing process began.

Amen

"Amen" is a Hebrew word meaning "yes" or "agreed". When we pray with others we say "Amen" when we agree with a prayer and don't say "Amen" if we disagree or are not sure. When we pray alone "Amen" is like a signature at the end of a letter. When others pray or make statements, saying "Amen" is like signing their letter. Saying "Amen" should not be automatic or thoughtless. Amen does not mean "uh-huh" or "whatever". It means "yes". We are responsible before God to listen carefully to what people say or pray and agree or not agree.

Angels

The natural and supernatural parts of reality interface. Angels (Malachi) are messengers of God to people. People see angels in a variety of ways: fire, a voice, a person with or without wings. The supernatural works into the natural in unpredictable ways. Most people experience angels, sometimes without knowing it. Angels can manifest physically, influencing physical space and even eating with people. Angels bring the supernatural into the natural for teaching, warning, encouragement, announcement. It is good to be receptive to the messengers of God. When you bring God's Word and Grace to people you serve like an angel.

Anger and Paranoia

Many of us are troubled with attacks of angry and paranoid thoughts and feelings which are only partly rational. These can fill our mind with a dark or fiery cloud that makes life miserable and lonely. These thoughts are never loving or productive. It is wrong, although very tempting, to follow these thoughts and develop them. We are forbidden to worry about this. We can wear ourselves out with the struggle. Why not do something instead? Bring them to Jesus and let Him do something. He will protect, heal, forgive, comfort and accept you. Try it. God bless you.

Attachment and Freedom

There once was a man who knew from faith and experience all his life that desire and attachment bring suffering. His hope was that after many lifetimes he might attain liberation by realizing absolute oneness. Then the uncreated creator, one and many, met him and promised to give him a new self. The uncreated creator emptied himself into the man and he became a new and other centered self. Then he awakened and realized he could have desire for Truth and attachment to loved ones without suffering for eternity. His liberation was a gift, not an attainment.

Be at Peace or Don't Care?

We are forbidden to worry or be anxious about anything and promised God's Peace about everything. Sometimes being at peace leads to not caring anymore or disengaging. How can we be at peace about our job or health or a struggle in our family or Church and remain engaged and effective? This is a special energy from the Holy Spirit, a passive activity, a restful urgency, a dynamic passivism, faith and works married in the Christian life. Ask for this experience and look for it. Resting in the Lord gives us energy to serve.

Beauty

The dictionary tells us that beauty is attractiveness, mostly to the eyes but also in usefulness or convenience. This kind of beauty is completely subjective to the individual or culture. The Bible contextualizes beauty with holiness or what is attractive to God: humility, faithfulness, obedience, service. Jesus was not physically attractive on earth and is completely and eternally beautiful. Beauty that is not attractive to God will end. Beauty that belongs in God's Kingdom is eternal. We can make and do things that are beautiful in both ways. Always see everything in the context of eternal beauty and life.

Blasphemy

Cursing or using God's name in stupid ways is not good. As a habit they are destructive infections in our language. Blasphemy has the deeper and more subtle meaning of using God's name or character for our own vanity. If we say "God said or told me" about what we imagine or hope it can be like signing God's Name to something we make up. This is forgery and can be manipulative. We create God in the image of our own imagination. Blasphemy is false prophecy that creates confusion about God in the community of His People. Avoid blasphemy.

Calling

There are ordinary, general callings, which Christians have in common and specific callings to each of us. The ordinary callings, giving order to our lives, is to believe in Jesus, become God's child, love each other and bear the fruits of the Spirit. Special callings are being married, studying medicine or plumbing, holding an office in the Church, being a faithful employee, going on missions, starting an NGO. If concentrating on a special calling interferes with loving each other, we lose touch with the ordinary calling and our lives go out of order. Keeping first things first brings blessing.

Cause and Effect

God made the universe with a law of cause and effect and sustains that law. If a Christian and a non-Christian jump off a building they will both fall down, not up. If you make your own morals and identity (eat from the fruit of the tree of the knowledge of good and evil), you will die. When people experience the consequences of their choices the Bible often says, "God did it." because cause and effect are from Him. Our participation in history and responsibility for our actions are not eliminated by God sustaining cause and effect.

Chance

God built the function of cause and effect into the creation. We cannot completely observe or understand cause and effect. In human observation many things happen by chance in that they are unpredictable. Chance is not a motivator or cause of events. Events take place through chance and through time but not by chance or time. If we flip a coin 10 times, we might perceive a tendency towards heads or tails. Over time and continuing coin flips the tendency disappears. Nothing happens by chance. Things happen by the Will of God and the will of His personal creatures.

Christian Patriotism

How can we Christians love our countries? We can pray for the leaders, even if they persecute us. Treasure and fight for our marriages. Commit random acts of kindness. Take control by going the second mile. Bless our neighbors by word and action in the Name of Jesus. Light even a small candle rather than make loud curses against the darkness. Build exemplary reputations for hard work, helpfulness, and dependability. Pray and look for ways to be part of the solution rather than part of the problem. Depend on God, ourselves and each other rather than government aid.

Christianity is Ordinary

Coming to believe in Jesus Christ and being born again was the most special thing that had ever happened in his life. He was very excited and tried to repeat the thrilling experience and emotion. This took a lot of effort and sometimes he had to pretend to himself and others. Gradually he realized the special things didn't give the order and stability he needed. The Ordinary, faithful values and habits of Christianity became the dependable foundation for his life. Special experiences are proper for special occasions. The Ordinary things give constant, faithful goodness to our lives.

Citizenship in Heaven

They told the little boy there was a present for him, kept high up in the closet. On his birthday he will not climb up in the closet to get it. It will be brought to him. Our citizenship is kept for us in heaven. We will not go to heaven to get it. When Jesus appears and God's Kingdom comes, He will bring it to us here on earth. God's Kingdom is His Will. We should live so that His Kingdom comes in our hearts, lives and relationships more and more each day while we wait.

Civil Disobedience

Civil disobedience is an option in the Christian life, but it is questionable and needs careful clarity. Praying for those in authority over us is commanded and not questionable ever. In any situation we can be militantly active in praying and informing those in authority that we are supporting them in that way. Civil disobedience is sometimes appropriate. It is always appropriate to take a stand for God by asking Him to take a stand for us. Praying can lead and guide our actions. Acting instead of praying is always a mistake. Prioritize prayer and blessing the city.

Comfort

The comfort of God doesn't basically mean being warm and dry, well fed and healthy with a secure job. It is more that our sins are forgiven, we are acceptable to God and He keeps us and holds us in His arms by his gentle power. We all have various troubles and anxieties. It is wise to ask God for His comfort and give ourselves to his embrace like the prodigal son. God wants to comfort us. If we ask for it, we know we will receive it because it is what He wants. Stay close and trust God.

Communion

Communion is a family meal that believers in Jesus share for remembering the incarnation and sacrifice of Jesus and for fellowship. Eating and drinking are ordinary things and basic to human life. Jesus didn't give us natural things like spring water and wild berries but artistic things – bread and wine. We add our creative work of dominion to what God has created and bring what we make to the meal. The meal is only for those who recognize the power of the body and blood of Jesus and their own need of them for forgiveness, healing and new life.

Controversial

Many Christians and others fear saying or doing anything controversial and warn against it. If something is not controversial it is universally accepted. Very little is universally accepted. Perhaps we agree about gravity and day following night, but not the flatness or the age of the earth. Nothing is more controversial than the Gospel of Jesus Christ. Christians should be peace makers but should not pretend there is peace when there isn't. Controversy cannot be avoided and will be with us until Jesus appears. Faith is trusting God when our situation is not safe, not pretending it is safe.

Covenant

A covenant is like a job offer from the Owner of a company. The Owner offers belonging, protection, community, insurance, productive work, and retirement plan. The Owner gives Himself in ethical principles, which express Himself and gives us the work of spreading His Truth all over the world. Our part is to believe that the Owner and company are good and true and faithfully commit ourselves to living within the company guidelines. Trying to live in the company by other principles won't work. We cannot keep the covenant perfectly, but Jesus has, and we can share in His perfection.

Culture

Culture is cultivating or growing things together and developing what we value. We have cultures of family, sport, business, nation. There are cultures of life and death, hope and despair, the Kingdom of God and of this world, love and selfishness. Christians are called to be aware of the culture around them and to contribute to it. Salt and light give flavor and clarity to the world. Being salt and light is blessing the city with the values of the Kingdom of God. Worshiping culture leads to a culture of death. Worshiping God leads to a culture of life.

Cyberspace

Cyberspace is a bit mysterious to most of us. So is the Supernatural part of reality. Life is hard and dangerous. Death is easy. Safety is not available in the physical world, cyberspace or the supernatural in themselves. We only find safety in Jesus and He is with us everywhere. When we spend time in Cyberspace (whatever that actually means) we need to remember Jesus, stay close to Him and include Him in our activities. We are always in God's presence and should not think of taking a break. We don't want God to take a break from us!

Draw Near to God

At the end of a dramatic personal testimony in Psalm 73, Asaph wrote "But as for me, it is good to draw near to God." God is always reaching from Heaven to be near us. We can draw near to Him by remembering Him and lifting ourselves up to Him, remembering He is always giving us life, protecting us, keeping us, enabling us. In the stress and struggles of life we can be stabilized and have a realistic perspective by remembering Him and His powerful Love for us. Be with Him day and night.

Earth, Air, Fire and Water

God loves the Earth and made us from it. The risen body of Jesus could be touched; it ate and worked. Through the Air comes the Wind of the Spirit, Who points us to Jesus, teaches us and gives us holy fruit. The breath of God gives us life. Fire is for cleansing, revealing or destruction. Fire shows the needle in the haystack of our sins. Water destroyed the earth once and now cleanses and refreshes us. Our God is sovereign over Earth, Air, Fire and Water and uses them to work His Will.

Entertainment and Education

Entertainment holds people between one active part of life and another in a suspended animation of enjoyment. Education is drawing people out and forward into fuller awareness, engagement, and learning. Entertainment can make education more pleasant but cannot replace it. Entertainment can be a blessing or enlargement for life. Education always is. Entertainment leaves people where they were. Education leads them forward. Entertainment gives the people what they want. Education gives the people what they need. Entertainment is cool. Education is hot. Entertainers can be popular and rich. Educators, believing in Jesus, bless and are blessed forever.

Equality

In many ways people are not equal: in health, intelligence, education, earning power, family background and inheritance. We are all equal in our need for God's Grace and salvation. Righteousness is like a balloon full of air. If you smash it with a big hammer it becomes a limp rag of rubber. If you just prick it with a tiny pin the same thing happens. In my need for God's forgiveness I am equal to a murdering mafia drug dealer. Some sins cause more damage than others but all of them bring death. We can't look down on anyone.

Fasting

The Bible assumes fasting as part of the Christian life. We can fast from food, conversation, reading, screen time, internet and other things. Fasting is usually for special purposes like repentance, thanksgiving, deciding on a job or a spouse, joining a Church, preparing for College. It can be for ourselves and/or for others. Fasting makes us weak and helps us know our need for God. Fasting sharpens the mind and helps us pray and receive God's guidance. Fasting is not magic and should not be a spiritual Olympics contest. It should not be overdone and damage our health.

Follow Your Heart

This is very popular advice. It expresses the humanistic belief that there is good inside everyone that can infallibly, authentically guide us in our lives if we look inside ourselves and find it. If the Bible is true, our hearts are deceptive and undependable and should not be trusted. We should trust in God's Word and test every impulse of our hearts by it. It is attractive to believe that what feels right is right. My feelings express "my truth", which isolates me from everyone else's truth. Your heart will tell you many things. Test them all.

Freedom to Fail

All Christians are sinners and broken. God intends us to be perfect and we are not, which is frustrating. When non-Christians fail their self-made identities can be shattered. When Christians fail, they can be forgiven and lifted up by Jesus. We don't want to fail at anything, but Jesus gives us freedom to fail without panic and move forward in hope and trust. When you fail, don't wallow in shame. Bring the failure to God openly in prayer. See the failure in the perspective of God's eternal Grace and Love. Receive His Peace, comfort and power for life.

Fundamentalism

Everyone is a fundamentalist and has foundation principles by which to understand the world and life. The fundamentals we claim and the fundamentals we live by are often different. It is fundamental to a humanist that people are good, to a post-modernist that people invent themselves, to a communist that equal distribution is more important than production, to a capitalist that freedom and funding are basic, to a Christian that Truth is revealed, to an atheist that Truth is not revealed but only discovered. What are the fundamentals of your life? Are you faithful to them or inconsistent?

Give Thanks in All Circumstances

Christians live in many different circumstances: health and sickness, wealth and poverty, safety and danger, popularity and isolation. The universal and eternal Truth of God's saving and living Gospel in Jesus Christ is what Christians have in common. This Truth works out in each different situation. Our circumstances, whether pleasant or unpleasant, can make us forget God's Love and be unthankful. God's Love surrounds all our circumstances. We should not be thankful for all circumstances because some are evil. If we remember God's Love, we can be realistically thankful, which is healthy and encouraging for us.

God's Law of Love

God's Law in the Sermon on the Mount is about loving relationships with each other. It is not about nationality, geography, diet, ceremonies, race, culture, or heritage. These things are valid parts of our Christian lives, but if they interfere with loving each other they become idolatry. We should not eliminate or ignore these things, but we should make sure they support and encourage loving each other. All the values and activities of our lives should serve love. Love belongs at the top of the hierarchy and gives meaning and life to everything else. Think love.

God's Promises

Many of God's promises are already fulfilled, either for people of long ago or for the whole community. They cannot be claimed by individuals. One promise that can be claimed by each of us is in Philippians 4:6-7. God promises that if we bring everything to Him, He will keep us in Christ Jesus. Our deepest need is to be wanted, kept and to belong. This is the promise we really need. This is the promise God always keeps for each of us. When we claim this promise our whole lives are cradled and sustained by God's Love.

Grace

He made damaging mistakes at work. His boss forgave him because he had hired him and trained him and hoped for him for the future. This is Grace, given by the powerful to the needy. By the power of the Holy Spirit we can give Grace to others. Weak, simple and despised Christians have the power from God to give grace to anyone. If Christians look at everyone through the lens of Grace, they become salt and light in the world and instruments of God's Peace. The weak hide behind their rights or supposed superiority. The strong give Grace.

Hallowed Be Thy Name

Someone's name is not only a label. It is also the character or reputation. "Hallowed be Thy Name" is not a complement or statement. It is a request that God's Name will be hallowed, or known as holy, on the earth. This is the first request in the Lord's Prayer because it is our greatest need. God's Name is often known as "myth" or "optional" or "fantasy". This mistake inhibits people from coming to Him. The main task of God's people from Abraham to the present is to live and speak so His Name is known as Holy.

Holy Selfishness

The couple decided to be more generous with their time, money, caring and praying. They gave more without expecting to be repaid. Then they discovered that their lives, peace and wellbeing increased. With God, you can't really give things away because they come back to you as blessings, seen and unseen, present and eternal. When we invest in the Kingdom of God, we are investing in ourselves with a certainty of a rich return. Those we bless become part of a rich crown of reward for us. When we are unselfish, God establishes our selves for us.

Hospitality

Welcoming strangers (Hospes) or enemies (Hostis) is a normal part of the Christian life. Christian hospitality is welcoming those who need a welcome and cannot pay us back. Giving parties for friends doesn't count. People can be welcomed into our houses, our time, our friendship. Hospitality is for fellow believers especially but also for unbelievers. Hospitality might be limited by special family needs for privacy. National hospitality in the Old Testament included conforming to Jewish religion and culture. We prepare a culture for visitors in our houses or communities. Visitors are not invited to shape our culture. Cultivate Xenophilia.

How We Know

Knowing what words mean and sharing those meanings is essential but not adequate for knowing truth. Knowing friends is more than knowing their name and its meaning. We know rationally, experientially, emotionally, socially and by revelation. If we expect too much of language, we will get frustrated. If we are not committed to what we say we will get sloppy and unstable. Language must be faithfully treasured and used in context with other ways of knowing. All our various ways of knowing are founded and supported on the fact that God knows us. Knowing begins with God.

I Don't Know

One of the great freedoms of Christianity is the freedom to say, "I don't know". People who don't have God's peace feel pressure to know everything and be right all the time. People feel shame in not knowing but the real shame is in pretending to know. We need to know Jesus, which isn't only an intellectual or rational way of knowing. You cannot seek wisdom unless you know you don't have it. Not many people are attracted to a know it all. The more you realize you don't know the faster you learn and gain wisdom.

"I Know What I Like."

Every life form knows what it likes. Most of our liking doesn't make sense and is not rational. We can pretend to like something because we are "supposed to like it". Not liking something doesn't mean we don't understand it or appreciate it. If someone likes something we don't, it doesn't make sense to us. They might not be able to tell us why they like it. To like is to enjoy or be attracted. We enjoy sin or we wouldn't do it. Liking tells us something about ourselves, not something about what we like.

Information

Information is mysterious. We don't know exactly what it is, but no one doubts that it exists. Information controls matter, particularly genetic material, but there is no evidence that matter produces information. Materialists have faith that matter produces information. It is more likely that information is supernatural, coming from God, who holds everything together by the power of His Word. In the beginning was the Word. In the beginning was information. The Word became flesh and lived with us. We don't understand this, but we can be thankful and trust in this Truth. It is the best explanation for everything.

Investing in Prayer

Normally, investment always involves risk, whether we invest in companies or personal relationships. In prayer there is a risk that we won't get what we want or become confused. But there is no risk that God will not bless us and make our lives more real when we pray. Prayer is treasure. Where our treasure is our hearts are also. When we invest in other people by praying for them our heart attitudes toward them change because we have invested in them. Try praying for people who are difficult or annoy you and see what happens.

Jesus is the Answer

Children in Sunday School learn that "Jesus" is a good guess in answering most questions. Actually, there is a great truth in that. The meaning of the Creation, the Flood, the Tower of Babel, the calling of Abraham and the history of the Jews, the Law of the Old Testament and human life in general is only in Jesus. When we understand Jesus we understand everything else. Jesus is the center of everything and gives everything meaning. The center is not a point or self-centered circle but a Cross and a Person – radiant and embracing.

Justice and Love

Justice and Love are very similar to each other. In the Bible "just" doesn't only mean fair or equal. It means fitting and appropriate. A justified angle fits the window frame. A justified person fits the frame of God's character and belongs with Him. Love is choosing to act into the loved one's life in ways that encourage and support their becoming who God wants them to be in His image. Justice and Love belong and work together. It is hard to imagine having one without the other. Jesus justifies us by His Love. Live like Jesus.

Learning from Our Emotions

God made our emotions. They are precious and we learn a lot from them. They are also broken and twisted by sin and often lie to us. Our emotions teach us a great deal about ourselves – our appetites and tastes and fears and pleasures. Emotions and experiences are half of truth. The other half is fact and meaning, which are both independent of and complimentary to our emotions and experiences. To kill our emotions is to kill ourselves. To equate our emotions with God's Word and Truth is to know good and evil and die.

Limits of Freedom

My freedom to swing my fist ends at your nose. My freedom of speech ends at lying and slander. When we understand, and respect the forms of mechanics, physics and aerodynamics we become free to fly across the ocean. If we ignore or violate the forms, we crash. If we go outside the forms God gives us for life, we move toward death. We choose some limits. Some are made by God or the society we live in. If we try to live only within the limits we choose for ourselves we will destroy ourselves and others.

Love and Trust

God loves us and we can trust Him for all he has actually promised but not for what we have imagined. The effect of God's love for us depends on our receiving it. We must always love our neighbors. Trust is different. Everyone is broken and distorted by their sin and that of others. We must trust others in hope and within the limits of their brokenness. We must not expect too much. If someone is kleptomaniac, we should love them and not trust them to overcome the disease immediately. Unwise trust can make things worse.

Loving Our Neighbor is Loving God

Once upon a time there was someone who believed in God and wanted to love Him. So, they began to read the Bible and go to Church and practice religious disciplines. They were militantly zealous for God's Truth, talking about it a lot and correcting anyone who had any misunderstanding. They tried hard to be a model of religious uprightness. But there was a hollow place in their heart. Then they began to love God by loving and serving their neighbors and the hollow place was filled up with deep, quiet, and energizing joy.

Luck

Many people don't believe in God. I sometimes say "God bless you" to them anyway because I believe in God and that He can bless them. Many people say "Good luck" to me although I don't believe in luck or chance. Chance always works out 50-50 so nothing happens by chance. People think of luck as the forces of an impersonal mechanical universe moving their lives around or as personalized "lady luck". The hope or wish for good luck is hopeless and random. We live in a personal reality where God sees and cares about everything. God bless you.

Male and Female

The idea that people are male, and female limits our freedom. The idea that gravity only pulls toward the earth also limits our freedom. Our limitations define and identify us as much as our possibilities do. If there are no limitations, there is no identity. The Bible says that God made His Image male and female as a default program. Biological and genetic science confirm the genetic polarity of animals. The Bible and Science agree. Gender is something that is given to us, not something we choose or invent. Imaginative gender alternatives are social or psychological constructs.

Meaning of Meaning

Meaning means relationships. That means that nothing has meaning in itself. The meaning of the color red is not in the color red, but in its relationships with green, blue, yellow, etc. The meaning of Adam in the creation account was pointedly not in himself (it is not good for the man to be alone). The meaning of Adam is in his relationships with God (which is not enough) and also with Eve. The meaning of Jesus is not in Jesus but in His relationships with the Father and the Holy Spirit. Meaning is a function of love.

Migration

1. We enter life through birth and live in a condition of death because of sin. 2. Then we can pass from death to life through belief in Jesus Christ. 3. Then we pass from life to death through natural death. 4. Then we pass from death to life with the appearing of Jesus and the restoration of everything. Everyone goes through phases 1 and 3. Phases 2 and 4 are open options provided by God. Some decline phases 2 and 4, which is very sad. Where are you in this process? Be sure not to skip any of the phases.

Mistrust

Trust is precious, powerful and fragile. Trusting God is foundational to the Christian Faith and life. The devil is constantly attacking trust to destroy it. He says, "Has God said?" "Make these stones into bread". "Jump off a building and make God prove Himself trustworthy." The thing to pray and work against during the Covid virus pandemic is the mushrooming of mistrust. Trust is the foundation of societies and economies. A threat against trust is a grave danger for all of us. Make an effort to be trustworthy in what you do and say. Be part of the solution.

Needy

There once was a man who was a Christian and knew a lot about Christianity. He had ups and downs in life and brought them all to God in prayer. One day he was struck by a heavy depression that weighed him down and made him hopeless and cynical. He cried out to God in his desperate and confused need. Gradually he experienced that his desperate need was poverty of spirit. The more he realized his poverty of spirit, the more of the Kingdom of God he had in his life. God can use anything to bless His children.

Nothing is Safe

The woman's highest priority was safety and security. She thought her job was secure but saw people around her losing theirs. She thought her bank was safe but read about scandals and failures. She thought her Church was safe, but people fought and gossiped and competed. She thought her health and life insurance policies were secure but there were complications. She felt horribly that nothing and no one could be trusted. Then she remembered that Jesus had proven His trustworthiness by dying for her and promised to be with her always. Standing on this foundation she could face everything else.

Ocean

In Mesopotamian myth Ocean controlled chaos; creating, surrounding and containing earth and sea. Also called serpent it gives birth to dragons. In the temple of Solomon, the Sea was the largest and only asymmetrical object. It was absurdly impractical as a washing vessel. The sea or Ocean is entirely contained and controlled by the temple or Kingdom of God. In Ezekiel's very detailed vision of the Temple the sea is not mentioned and in Revelation the sea is said to be no more. God is greater than all people's myths and imaginations and swallows them up in victorious control.

One, Two or Three?

If "all is One" all relationships are evil and unreal. If all is two there is no subjectivity, only duality. It was not good for Adam to be alone because "God alone is God and God is not alone". Only the God of the Bible is a reasonable basis and explanation for the reality we experience. God is Love because He is Three and loves among Himself. There is goodness in our evil and crumbling world because of God. Trust in Him, Father, Son and Holy Spirit. Worship and obey Him alone. Accept no counterfeit substitutes.

Our Brother's Keeper

Many Christians have been stressed under the weight of being their brother's keeper. God did not tell Cain he was his brother's keeper. Cain knew that only God can keep us, so he was cynically asking "Am I God to my brother?". Everyone makes their own responses and lives with the consequences. Our responsibility is to love our brother and pray God to keep them. We must care for each other, support and pray for each other, but not keep each other. We are not our brother's keeper – it is hard enough to be their brother.

Parable of a victim

Once upon a time there was a man who had various personal and business difficulties. He had been taught that he was a victim and had rights and entitlements. He wondered why God didn't give him what he deserved. The idea that he might be guilty of anything seemed an intolerable burden of debt. Then he realized that he could afford to be guilty because Jesus had already paid for everything. He could face his own responsibility for his life freely and realistically, knowing the weight of any amount of guilt could be lifted from him. The healing began.

People are Good

We need goodness in our lives and in our world. This prompts people to declare and believe they and other people are good. This is a dangerous fantasy, like declaring that poisonous snakes are safe. If people are good, they don't need Jesus, which is a terrible, deadly lie. We need perfect and absolute goodness. Sadly, people are not good enough, but happily God is. Only God is good and the measure of goodness, not our taste, pleasure or comfort. Because God is all good and all powerful, He can make us good if we let Him.

Personal Goodness

In our day humanists teach us that we should value our natural goodness and have self-respect. The Apostle Paul teaches us that our goodness or righteousness is like filthy rags. True goodness is available to us from Jesus Christ. We can be truly good in Him and have realistic hope and joy and thankfulness. Goodness and life do not come from the natural created world or from our natural selves but from the Creator. If we are humble and poor in spirit, we can receive all we need for goodness and life from Jesus. Trust in Him and be glad.

Prayer and Bicycle Riding

Once there was a teenager who read lots of books and websites about bicycle riding. They felt that they knew all about it. One day they got on a friends' bicycle to ride it and fell off. They realized true knowledge involves doing. Later they read lots of books and websites about praying and loving their neighbors and felt they knew a lot about it. They started a blog about prayer and many people joined the discussion. They began to feel lonely and isolated and realized they needed to actually pray and love people in person.

Predestination

God makes choices in eternity that effect all of time. He sees and knows time from the beginning to the end because He made it. He has known all of us since before we were born. His foreknowledge and predestination work together. We make choices in time and are always invited to choose God. From the perspective of time we can always live in hope. We know that God has chosen or predestined us when we choose Him, which we could not do without His help and personal calling. If we choose Him, He will accept us. Choose God.

Pride

Why is the Bible so negative about pride? It is good and healthy to be pleased and encouraged by our abilities and accomplishments. Pride can be shallow, like pride in my eye color or skin texture, which are not abilities or accomplishments. Pride can be vain, which means empty or worthless. It is natural to be proud, while it is spiritual to be thankful. Pride in others can be good but a person who "is proud" is self-centered, self-dependent and imploding. The devil is proud and dead and wants us to be too. Jesus is humble and powerfully alive.

Questions as Blessings

When talking to unbelieving friends and relatives about Jesus, Christians often make statements and recount experiences. While these can be true it is easy to say "no" to them. It is harder to say "no" to a question. Questions go under the radar and give the Holy Spirit an entrance to work in the person's mind and heart. Ask questions about meaning, purpose, identity as a gift and give space for thought. When people begin to ask you back, preach Christ because they are hungry. Questions stimulate appetite. Pray for effective questions to ask. Love your neighbors.

Race

Race doesn't seem to be a factor in the Kingdom of God. God loves everyone. Everyone needs God. God seems to be color blind. God is the great leveler: The rich are poor; the poor are rich. Color, family history, education, religious background, political views, entitlements, or privileges don't seem to make much difference. We are not saved or lost by our background, only our foreground. We are all the same to Jesus. To think differently causes problems. Healing can be painful and frightening. Let us allow the Holy Spirit to form this understanding in our hearts and minds.

Reading and Listening

It is very difficult to read or listen clearly because our own expectations and assumptions muddy the waters. When people speak and we basically hear ourselves, conversation is impossible, and we end up lonely and alienated. When we read into a text instead of out of it, we also end up talking with ourselves. Love is other centered. If we sacrifice our agendas and concentrate on the other, understanding will grow and both of us will be blessed. We don't need to agree with what we hear or read but we need to look away from ourselves.

Relevant

Is the Bible relevant to our culture and society? This question assumes that our culture and society are the measure of truth and reality and wonders if the Bible can be made to fit in. Christianity is radical and assumes that the Bible describes truth and reality. The values of the Bible are absolute and eternal, while alternative values of any human culture are relative and temporary. If the Bible is true, we should measure our culture against it, not the other way around. Are your personal and social cultures relevant to the Kingdom of God? Think about it.

Religion or Idolatry

Over time, Christians have developed various ways of responding to God's salvation, which we can call religion. These include architecture, liturgies, rites, ceremonies, traditions, paintings, sculptures, windows, special clothing, creeds, catechisms, music, and other things. God is Love. The Gospel of Jesus Christ is Love. We need to think and pray about how all our religious practices direct and support us in loving each other. If they do, they are a blessing for us. If they don't, they can be a distracting idolatry or escape. Don't abandon religion but make sure it is actually a blessing for you.

Religion

Religion is either a system of activities intended to connect a person with absolute truth or a faithful devotion to some basic principles (like communism). It usually involves the supernatural. The basis of Christianity is God connecting Himself with us through His Word in the creation, the incarnation of Jesus Christ, the Bible and the activity of the Holy Spirit. Christianity starts with God coming to us, not us trying to reach God, so it is different from religion. It all starts with God's Love. It doesn't start with our efforts or system. Let yourself be found by God.

Restrictions

More and more, people are offended by restrictions and claim increasing freedom in life, especially in identifying themselves. When someone gets the freedom to drive a car they must learn and observe many strong restrictions. Freedom from the restrictions will cause death to the driver and others. Freedom to use human language requires submitting to many restrictions or communication will not happen. Restrictions shape the lively truth of our freedoms. God gives us many restrictions in the Bible. These are not for making life smaller but for making life possible and clearly defined. Accept God's restrictions and live.

Revelation

Some of the events in the book of Revelation take place on earth and some in heaven (the supernatural dimensions of reality). The ones on earth take place in time, while the ones in heaven take place in eternity. "A day is like a thousand years and a thousand years is like a day" describes the relationship between time and eternity. Can we expect to measure the events in heaven with a calendar? Probably not. The events are true and real even though we cannot fully imagine or measure them. We live by faith and not by sight.

Righteousness

A "right angle" (90 degrees) is right because it fits into the window or door frame. Becoming righteous is being reshaped to fit into God's Kingdom and become more in His Image. We should work in obedience to become more fitting. This is the small part of the process of becoming righteous. The big part is God's part in giving us a new heart and a right spirit, cleaning us from the distortions of sin by the blood of Jesus and guiding and encouraging us by His Holy Spirit. Trust in God's part so you can do your part better.

Risk and Trust

The wealth of nations and all good relationships are built on trust. With trust there is usually risk: The stock might crash, the company might downsize, the spouse die, the friend change, the Church split. It is good to analyze the risks and be realistic about our hopes and expectations. We can dare to trust and risk if our lives are founded and framed by the promises of God to save and keep us. In this there is zero risk. God will not die or fail or change. Live in focus with the one risk free relationship.

Self-Referential

Self-Referential is often thought of as a positive value, especially in art. Actually, self-referential is another way of saying sin and death. God is absolutely and eternally other referential. The reference of Jesus is not Himself but the Father and the Spirit. Adam and Eve were made other referential. Their references were God and each other. They became self-referential by knowing good and evil for themselves, independently. God is Love. Love is other-referential. Life is only in God and Love. Allow the Holy Spirit to make you more and more other-referential and receive more and more life from God.

Spiritual Activities

The resurrected and glorified Jesus Christ is our only example of the true spiritual life. What did He do? He ate and drank (Luke 24:36-44, Acts 1:4). He taught history (Luke 24:13-27). He worked, created and practiced hospitality (John 21:4-13). Eating, drinking, teaching, working, being creative and practicing hospitality are all spiritual activities for the Christian. Natural activities become spiritual by connection with the supernatural through prayer, thankfulness and God's blessing. The religious or ceremonial part of our spiritual lives belongs with the other parts, which are equally real and spiritual. Spiritual means totally real, healed, not divided.

"Spiritual" Connections

Many people ask and wonder if various events and circumstances have a "spiritual" or supernatural connection. Two questions might help think this through: Is there anything that you do or that happens to you that God is not interested in? Is there anything that you do or that happens to you that the devil is not interested in? We are connected with the supernatural part of reality 24/7. Prayer is always indicated. We don't need to be in vague confusion or worry. We are always in a battle and should always include God in our situation. Pray constantly.

Test Everything

In I Thessalonians Paul teaches us to test everything in order to avoid putting out the Spirit's fire and holding prophecies in contempt. If we only say "yes" to everything that claims to be a prophecy and every emotion and experience that comes to us, we go out of focus with God's Truth. The result of testing should be first holding on to all that is good so we can identify what is evil. If we test to identify evil, it will not help us to know the good. The purpose of testing is to increase our love.

Testing and Tempting

Testing (Dokimazo in Greek) looks for the good. Tempting (Peirazo in Greek) looks for the bad. Sometimes these words are translated in the same way. God is always testing us to prove and demonstrate that our faith is strong and that we have grown as His children. We should test each other to find out what is good. We are tempted to tempt each other to find out what is bad, so we feel better. Show people how good they are and encourage them to be better with God's help. Build people up, don't tear them down.

The Desires of Our Hearts

"Delight yourself in the Lord and He will give you the desires of your heart." Ps. 37:4. "Earth has nothing I desire besides you." Ps. 73:25. This is a very great promise. There is a lot of discussion about which desires of our hearts we can expect to get from God. The text makes it obvious. What we desire is what we delight in, so God is promising to give us Himself. If we get little and have God, we are rich. If we get much and don't have God, we are poor. Treasure God.

The End is Near!

Many Christians are interested in and concerned about the End Times. People ask, "Are we in the End Times?" Yes, we are, ever since John wrote Revelation. He also wrote that we are in the "Last Hour" 2000 years ago. The End of the world is near! "End" doesn't mean "finish" but fulfillment or reaching the goal. God will bring the world or earth to the fulfillment of His purpose in creating it. The End is near actually means the Beginning is near – the Beginning of the fulfillment of God's Kingdom on earth. Your Kingdom come!

The Parable of the Mother and the Boy

Once upon a time there was a woman who had a little boy. She loved the boy and knew that he would touch the hot stove in the kitchen. She begged and scolded him and pleaded with him not to touch the stove. When he did touch the stove one day it was not her fault. She hurt for him. Her knowledge that he would touch the stove did not take away his significance and responsibility. When the boy was sorry he had disobeyed his mother, she kissed him and forgave him.

The Problem of Evil

If God is all good and all powerful, why is there evil? This question cannot be answered unless people are assumed to be responsible change agents. God didn't make us automatically good, but with the responsibility of choosing good. Often, we don't, and evil happens. History is linear and accumulative. Evil builds up and effects everyone. We are not guilty of what happens to us, only of what we choose and do. People tend to think of evil as "them". If God would do something to get rid of all evil, what would happen to you?

The Problem of Good

If God is all powerful and all good, why is there evil in the world? If it were not for the goodness of God, we wouldn't know what evil is. Everything would just be normal and natural like volcanoes, beautiful sunsets, and poisonous snakes. A more useful question is: If everything is cooling down and tending toward chaos, why is there good? Nature is not good or bad – it just is what it is. Good and evil are supernatural energies working into nature. Good is original, beginning with God. Evil is a distortion which God is correcting.

The Spirit Blows and Hovers

"Spirit" means "wind" in Hebrew and Greek in the Bible. The Wind is a Person with a Will and a Purpose. The Wind hovers like a dove over the waters of creation, the flood and the baptism of Jesus – three new beginnings. The Wind blows and breathes into us Truth, Wisdom, rebuke, guidance, comfort and the Name of Jesus. He is the Spirit of Jesus Christ, proclaiming Him and pointing to Him as our Savior and Guide in life. The Spirit enters into us, plants seeds and bears fruit. We should treasure and love Him more.

The Temple of the Holy Spirit

God is the God of relationships and not self-centered. He wants us to be the same in His Image. The temple of the Holy Spirit and the body of the bride of Christ are not about us as individuals but about us as a family or community, children of God together. Where two or more are together Christ and His Spirit are present in a more complete way than when we are alone. We can pray alone, and the Spirit blesses us individually, but our eternal life is not singular. Practice now for eternity.

Trust and Confidence

In times of crises and stress like the Coronavirus pandemic of 2020, it is hard to trust. Governments make mistakes, anyone we meet might infect us, those who control our online life have various agendas. We cannot see or understand all details. But we can see the big picture in God's Person and promises. He promises to keep us so nothing can separate us from Him. All the confusing and stressful details of our lives have their true meaning in the perspective of God's eternal promises. Keep your eyes on Jesus. Think about His power and faithfulness and be at peace.

Trust and Panic

Christians live in a peaceful atmosphere of trust because of the faithful power of God our savior. We do not live in a paranoid miasma of conspiracy panic. All authority comes from God but is never used perfectly. Governments make mistakes. We are to be wise as serpents and gentle as doves. We are to give God what is God's and give Caesar what is Caesar's. We are not to condemn each other for drawing the line in different places. Christians are to bless the city so that it will be a blessing to live in it.

Two Kinds of People

There are only two kinds of people on the earth – those who know their need of God (the poor in spirit) and those who don't (the rich in spirit). The rich depend on themselves, their careers and accomplishments, their societies and traditions for their identity and meaning. The poor depend on God in Christ. Both groups include wealthy and poor, attractive and unattractive, admirable and despised, religious and less religious, healthy and sick, beautiful and ugly. We tend to judge by appearances and our taste. God judges by the heart. Be poor in spirit and live.

Unconditional Love

Emotions change under different internal and external conditions. Love is much bigger than emotions. Love is the choosing to act and be available to support the loved one in becoming who God wants them to be. God is constantly and perfectly available and acting to make us truly in His image. The effectiveness of God's Love and our love depends on the condition of the loved one's willingness to accept it. Emotions can support or inhibit true love. Love is not something that happens to us. It is something we choose. Work to choose love under all conditions.

Understanding God's Word

Language is difficult. It is probably impossible to describe with words in space and time things and events that take place mostly in eternity. There are three heavens: where the birds fly, where the stars turn and the supernatural. One word is used for all of them. The text itself doesn't say enough – it needs to be explained. Precision is limited and never perfect. If we needed more precision, God would give it to us. We cannot understand God's Word adequately only with our mind. God's Word is the Bible, the creation and Jesus. True understanding is a holistic relationship.

Value and Desire

Desire increases perceived value immediately. Where your heart is, there will be your treasure also. You will invest yourself in what you want. We can follow the natural desires that come and go, or we can learn to desire what God desires for us and be stable in His Truth and Love. If we want what God wants all our other desires and values come into their proper place and focus. With us this is impossible, but we can ask God to help us want what He wants, and He will do it. Desire what God desires.

Victory During Covid

Not all things are good. In all things God works for good for those who love Him. Let's look for and receive God's victory in our lives during Covid. Because of the restrictions, does the Holy Spirit teach you to treasure and develop relationships? Does He teach you patience, faithfulness and kindness? The Covid pandemic will end. God's victories in our lives will not end. Rejoice! We can ask God to end the virus. God does not give us everything we want. He gives us everything He wants, which is much better. Love God and let Him love you.

Wanting What God Wants

God has promised that if we ask for what He wants us to have He will give it to us. It is clear God wants us and everyone to grow in the fruits of the Spirit and the values of the Beatitudes and to love each other. It is not clear God wants us to be healed or get the job or the visa or pass the test. What else do we know from Scripture that God wants for us and others? Ask for what God wants and everything else will come into focus in His Kingdom.

What About Those Who Have Never Heard? (Part I)

Many tender-hearted Christians worry about those who have never heard the Gospel, read the Bible or met a missionary. The basic thing anyone needs to know to be saved is that they are broken and need God to forgive and fix them. God tells everyone this in various ways: The Bible, conscience, dreams, the Holy Spirit's conviction. The question is how people respond. In Romans 1 we read no one has an excuse. It is urgent to give people more opportunities to respond by missionary work near and far. Encourage poverty of spirit.

What About Those Who Have Never Heard? (Part II)

Knowing that we need God is essential for salvation. Anyone who knows this and reaches out to God will be saved. Having a Bible and hearing the Gospel is not enough. God has various ways of letting people know they need Him: The Bible, other people, the creation that shows how inconsistent and unfaithful we are, conviction by the Holy Spirit. God does not control peoples' response. Some reject Him, though God tells everyone they need Him. It is important that they hear about God's Truth and Love through Jesus Christ from us.

Why?

"Why?" is often a very agonized cry. Why me? Why this? Why now? We want to have a cause and effect understanding. When people asked Jesus, in John 9, why a man was born blind He basically said "don't look back for a reason, look forward for a purpose." We put ourselves more in focus with God's Kingdom and purpose when we ask "How will God use this for good in the lives of those who love Him?" "Why?" can be an expression of hopelessness because we know we won't find out. "What for?" expresses hope and trust.

Wisdom

Once there was a very intelligent, educated and gifted pastor. He knew the Bible and could teach it well. The Church profited from his work and service. One day he welcomed an older woman into the Church. She was not very intelligent or educated or skilled. She spent much of her time praying for people, encouraging and helping them as she could. Through fellowship with this woman, the pastor also became gradually more wise by her example and encouragement. Intelligence has value but without wisdom, not full value. Wisdom without intelligence has full value. We learn from each other.

Words and Feelings

Once upon a time there was a child who had strong and confusing feelings about many things. No one could actually share their feelings and they could not express them intelligently. Then someone helped them to use words faithfully and clearly to express themselves and understand their feelings. When the subjective feelings had an objective partner in stable words, they became less disturbing and controlling and more enjoyable and useful. A marriage between mysterious feelings and clarifying words produces a child of peace for us. We can choose our words while we do not choose our emotions.

www.ingramcontent.com/pod-product-compliance
Lightning Source LLC
Chambersburg PA
CBHW050329120526
44592CB00014B/2110